Bypass

Bypass

Poems by

Dave Malone

© 2023 Dave Malone. All rights reserved.
This material may not be reproduced in any form, published,
reprinted, recorded, performed, broadcast,
rewritten or redistributed without
the explicit permission of Dave Malone.
All such actions are strictly prohibited by law.

Author photo by Jenni Wichern
Cover photo by Alexander Paul
Cover design by Shay Culligan

ISBN: 978-1-63980-392-7

Kelsay Books
502 South 1040 East, A-119
American Fork, Utah 84003
Kelsaybooks.com

For Bowie (2010–2023)

a mini-Schnauzer
whose courageous heart
and ear-shattering bark
were far from miniature

Other Books by Dave Malone

View from the North Ten

O: Love Poems from the Ozarks

You Know the Ones

Tornado Drill

Acknowledgments

Some of these poems, often in earlier versions, were first published elsewhere. Grateful acknowledgement to the editors of these journals.

Between These Shores Literary and Arts Anthology: "Sailing Elsewhere"

Delta Poetry Review: "Bury Me," "Dr. Abbott"

Dunes Review: "Knocking on Doors"

The Heartland Review: "Buzzards," the 2nd place award winner in the 2022 Joy Bale Boone Prize.

Innisfree Poetry Journal: "Constellations"

Midwest Zen: "Evening Walk"

MockingHeart Review: "Minutes from Signing the Papers"

The Orchards Poetry Journal: "Dusk Walk with My Mother"

Paddleshots: "Great Aunt"

Pilgrimage: "Champion"

Poppy Road Review: "The Good Work," "Night Snow in April"

Science Write Now: "For a Limited Time Only"

Slant: "The Last Supper"

Spindrift: "Artichoke Heart"

Tipton Poetry Journal: "Autumn Float"

Umbrella Factory: "Baseball Card"

"After I Disappointed a Friend" and "Brown Recluse" originally appeared in *Every Day Poems* (*tweetspeakpoetry.com/every-day-poems*).

"Spa Day" originally appeared on my Instagram, *@dave.malone*, on April 5, 2023.

* * *

I would like to thank Karen Kelsay, Delisa Hargrove, Peter Davies, Shay Culligan, Jenna V. Ray, and Julie Kelsay for giving this book life and a home. Thanks also to Paulette Guerin Bane whose expert editorial suggestions often knocked me out of my chair and improved a great number of these poems. And much gratitude to my writing challenge group. They are a force to be reckoned with, and because of their encouragement (and by providing good old-fashioned accountability), I composed much of this new work.

I am grateful to my literary patrons who just won't go away. Thank you. These amazing folks are: Allison A. deFreese, Amy Fischer, Axel Liimatta, Brian Katcher, Callie Feyen, Clara Applegate, Derek Dowell, Elizabeth Brixey, Emily Edwards-Long, Felix Lloyd, J. Kyle Johnson, Jason McCollom, Jessica Nease, Kathy Kirkaldie, Kimberly Allen, Lauren Campbell, Mike Luster, Nathanael Elbrecht, Neal and Betsy Delmonico, Rachel Cobb, Sarah Morris, Sharon Buzzard, Steve Wiegenstein, and Wayne Blinne.

Contents

I.

Knocking on Doors	19
The Last Supper	20
Great Aunt	21
The Makings of a Quarterback	22
Tom Sawyer	23
Ten-hut	24
Champion	25
Doll Heads	26
Until the Fourth of July	27
The Parent He Never Had	28
Mowers	29
Seeing the Bangles at Worlds of Fun in Kansas City in 1986	30
Practice	31

II.

Baseball Card	35
Partyin' with Saint Paul	36
Debate Teacher	37
College Road Trip to Minneapolis	39
For a Limited Time Only	40
Artichoke Heart	41
Spa Day	42
How I Love/Despise Your Instagram Summer	43
Dual Threats	44
History Professor	45
Terms	46
Constellations	47
Malus domestica	48
In the Breezeway	49

Family Reunion	50
My Grandfather's Concord Wine	51
Dusk Walk with My Mother	52

III.

Yard Sale	55
Olympic Rings	56
Next Door	57
Buzzards	58
The Good Work	59
Breakthrough	60
Frances	61
It Ain't Easy at the Top	62
Shaq Dancing	63
How to Lose Weight during a Pandemic	64
White Dwarf Star: A Love Poem	65
Forgotten Ice Cube Tray on the Counter	66
Pie	67
Young Couple	68
Colorado Wildflower Seed Mix	69
Brown Recluse	70
When Children Need Another Player and the Smallest Boy Asks	71

IV.

Bypass	75
Night Snow in April	76
Sailing Elsewhere	77
Casts	78
Town Lion, Standing Room Only	79
Flood	80

Big Muddy	81
I Love the Little Maple	82
Soccer Field	83
Minutes from Signing the Papers	84
Dr. Abbott	85
Daycare Playground	86
Swing	87
In Two Years' Time	88

V.

Driving Years Later	91
One Minute Read	92
Meditation on Fifty	94
After I Disappointed a Friend	95
What There Is to Know about the Human Heart	96
Symmetry	97
Cooking for a New Friend	98
Her Freckled Face Seen in a Batch of Bananas	99
Warn Your Doctor If You Get a Parasitic Infection When Taking This Drug	100
Skins	101
Autumn Float	102
Drinking Near Dark	103
Evening Walk	104
Bury Me	105
Country Farmhouses Like Mine	106

Mine was a Midwest home—you can keep your world.
—William Stafford

And they call this the Great Midwest.
Sure make a hell of a car.
And the old hearts, they race
their way through the night,
the upheaval of who they really are.
—John Mellencamp

I.

O youth whose heart is right . . . .
Wilt thou be true and just
And clean and kind and brave?
Well; but for all thou dost,
Be sure it shall not save.
—AE Housman

Childhood is an absolute
treasure house of imagination.
—John O'Donohue

Go back to your childhood.
What were the fascinating things?
What's beyond the stars?
It goes on always and always and always.
—Alan Watts

Knocking on Doors

We were fourteen or fifteen,
the lot of us. Kansas kids
two hours from home
in another lonesome burg.

It was March after a deep rain
that left the daffodils standing
at attention and town huts
silver in the gloaming.

Alone, I hoofed it back to the church
before the other pamphleteers.
Inside the temple rose the pleasant
musty smell of a tired air conditioner

battling first heat—such a scent
of surrender, hanging in the wet air,
an hour I owned before the evening
candles were lit.

The Last Supper

At sixteen I was asked
to preach at our country church
and lifted a sermon from my great uncle
who hand-crafted picture frames
in his garage and preached on the side.

He knew about loss, his wife murdered
in a botched grocery store crime,
and he was too weak to cast
the first stone, not even in Korea
on the ambulance crew

before coming back home
to solitude and his garage
where it was *The Last Supper*
he framed the most,
the sideways face of betrayal.

Great Aunt

Autumn morning too cold
for its own good. The day
she buries her last sister.

Behind the country church,
with her back to the timber,
she sits straight in a crooked
funeral chair, its feet dug in
like leaning fence posts.

Unpinned, her white hair floats
in the wind, never falling back
in place, and her blue eyes
leave the entourage, hide deep
in the brown ridge past the steeple.

Half-shelled acorns crunch
like old cow bones beneath my boots
as I approach to give condolences
to this blazing lamp so unlike
the ghost in the ground.

I want to tell her everything,
tell her, she has to live forever.
Never leave the farm.
Never leave
me.

The Makings of a Quarterback

In another life I was a quarterback—
the fluid arm cocked behind the head
to zip an arrow to target, the slot receiver best
served in the flat. That life's throws taught me

at ag camp by Danny, Kansas State's backup
who saw talent in me, unlike my father,
uncles, the men who pledged to matter most.
And in twilight hours, when the stadium

was hushed, Dan worked with me on form,
and how one's eyes must move like a doe's—
ever present yet relaxed—so the defense
will slip just like the dawn, awkward

and heavy in first light, and then you strike—
the spiral that surprises.

Tom Sawyer

> *A modern-day warrior*
> *Mean, mean stride*
> *Today's Tom Sawyer*
> *Mean, mean pride*
>   —Rush

You'd think the image of
his older brother beating
him down into a curling snake
would've stayed with me most. How the end
of the hallway framed both brothers
beneath a heaven-facing Jesus.

But no, I remember the thud of bare fists
on soft flesh, the elder's knuckles
smacking on small shoulders
sounding his discontent
of pains unknown
to middle schoolers.

Ten-hut

He was that blond-haired bully
in the movies. Twisting kids' arms behind
their backs to steal lunch money, their dignity,
their girlfriends, their parents' love.

Once in middle school, he beat up a kid
with his own bike. Then locked them both
to the rack. After he graduated high school,
he went into the army, became a major.

Last winter a childhood friend took out half
his colon, spilling out like rusted bike chains,
she said.

Champion

She was supposed to win
the spelling bee. She learned
their language as an outsider—
the Asian girl of that Nebraska town.

In seventh grade, she studied
Greek etymology, and Latin to boot.
And the village, they put their hope in her.
So the day arrived like none other.

Golden, horizon to horizon
like a wheat harvest their grandparents
once knelt down to. Yet she strung
them all up there on the stage.

It was *incendiary,* of course.

Doll Heads

The girl holds a doll head in her arms
like God cradling one long wiggly word,

or like the deepest breath, the wind
across the Sahara yet to be.

She surgically removes the dolls' tops
to reveal their empty insides,

the Pleiades,
the vacant black holes,

the equations Einstein penned
in dreams she made up.

On the porch, the female figures
stand sentry. One after another.

Cactus, succulent, lithops
sprouting from open heads.

Until the Fourth of July

The neighbor kids own skin
that glistens in gold
housed only in paintings
on family-famous slides
my dad fires up on holidays.

The neighbor kids tan
in summer months
and eat pounds of PB&J
beside the chilled water
of their swimming pool.

The neighbor kids don't walk
to the store, they glide above the landscape
like swans at English lakes
captured on Dad's slides—
all the places he said he'd take us.

The neighbor kids have it made
until the Fourth of July—
when our fireworks fizzle
in the calm of our wet lawn

while their father returns home
from a bender, his voice
booming louder than
any M-80 of his youth.

The Parent He Never Had

The devoted children
sprint into the dojo
on a Saturday.

The teacher yells at them
and most cower—
tan dogs hiding in their *karategi*.

Save the new girl.

She stands, hugs him.

Mowers

For kicks, the teenage boy
hikes black dress socks
to mid-calf then cranks up
the lawn mower.

He likes a good time,
drinking beer,
smoking an occasional joint,
skateboarding the arroyo,

and unseating church elders
with questions they can't answer,
*How is Gandhi, much better than I,
condemned to hell since he wasn't a Christian?*

At the mulberry, he cuts too close,
hacking a root, and the grinding blade
dies. In a far cul-de-sac, another mower
rumbles in this perfect neighborhood.

Seeing the Bangles at Worlds of Fun in Kansas City in 1986

"Manic Monday" played on every radio station,
from Goodland, Kansas, to Brooklyn that summer,

and my buddy Mike and I serpentined our way
past tweens with ice cream cones as big as their heads

to commandeer seats half an hour before the show
when no one was there, save a rented bodyguard

with a belly and a taser. Track-runner thin,
Mike flailed in our empty row and complained

about being early—he didn't believe in anticipation,
having a stepfather who robbed his family

of lunch money and weekends, so miracles or even the belief
that good shit will happen soon, was out of the question.

He took off for pop and pretzels though I didn't wait
long until they sang their big hit

that Mike never found his way back for.

Practice

In high school rich kids
composed the major notes
of the golf team roster.
When their metal drivers
connected with Ping's finest,
cymbals broke through silence,
moved onlookers to tears.

Outside this treble clef, a few
of us sang, the ragtag voices
of troubadours, knocking Top-Flites
to lips of greens, learning the skill
of the short game, bringing bass
into the lower clef.

One Sunday after church, my parents
drove us past the municipal course.
A friend with a steel driver in hand
stood inside a pelting storm
that made our windshield weep
and threatened electric death,

but there he was poised,
on the towering ninth hole.
His arms swept back, and he drove
an orange ball into the infinite gray,
to song only he must have heard.

II.

*Get out of here! Go back to Rome.
You're young and the world is yours . . .
Don't come back. Don't think about us.
Don't look back.*
—Alfredo, *Cinema Paradiso*

Baseball Card

When I was twenty-one, I worked
at a convenience store, the same
as any other. Coffee refills, gas,
fountain drinks fueled as if
by natural springs. One quiet Sunday,
I carted the trash to the dumpster
and stole a smoke break.

On top of the bin, nestled like robin eggs,
a pair of black bags had been delivered
by nearby duplex dwellers.
The herd of homeless had cracked
the top layer for food or clothes.
Clear of any wheeling beetles,
a baseball card lay prone
between bag and dumpster lip.

With bright blue eyes the player looked
off-camera. His last season's stats
showed improvement in his game
though his lifetime batting average
hovered on the precipice of this garbage bin,
revealing he couldn't hit over .250—
and I saw no reason to believe
he was a Gold Glove
capable of saving his career.

Partyin' with Saint Paul

I would've partied with Saint Paul.
Only in his college days, though.
Before the bloodletting. Before the blindness.
Before the letters. Before the sainthood.

I would have partied with Paul at the dorm.
Shotgunned beers beside bunk beds,
tipped trash can barrels at hallway ends
for tobacco-puck hockey, checked his body
and bad-ass beard into the bulletin board,
against the RA's picture and cleanliness requests.

I would have partied with that guy at the quarry.
Knocked back whiskies together on the edge.
Tossed pint bottles like stones into the abyss.
Yelled our desires across the expanse.
Talked about the significance of Ur,
the bull's lyre he swore strummed in his head
as sure as the rushing Cydnus.
Pondered our immediate futures,
him for the army, me for seminary.

Debate Teacher

She gave us medallions
with the words
"Forever Young"
inscribed in faux gold.

I thought it odd,
this phrase for us,
so young
we wanted only

to be older
and were too green to realize
she meant the pith
for herself.

She died last week.
Just 50.

The color photo
with the obit shows
her mahogany hair
tinged in white

like piano keys
on the grand
in the college auditorium
where one night

she asked us
to stop debating
climate change
and played that song

over the speakers,
as she bounced
across the stage
until we bounced back.

College Road Trip to Minneapolis

Joanfrost over lake,
I scribble in my journal
while a friend of a friend
drives a pensive quartet
in his rattling Chevy Nova
up pock-marked I-35
in the December dark.

From my backseat view,
moonlight casts slender trees
in outline like movie monsters
reprising their roles
in the nightmares my mother
could never save me from.

Through the farmlands' icy mist
a frozen catfish floats on the surface
of the pond, its iced whiskers
like running mascara beside a shore
adorned with yellow knifing grass,
and I know I suffocated Joan
with my midnight phone calls,
with my below-the-balcony
shrieking drama.

But how could she intuit
I was still nine years old,
breathing hard to catch up
to the car my mother left running
the night she disappeared into the snow,
the thinnest of apparitions.

For a Limited Time Only

On Sundays, my neighborhood smells
of laundry, lilac blooms running out
of vents in search of pasture.
In summer, air conditioners rumble
beneath cumulus painted skies. One fall,
the armadillos marched in. Fully loaded.
They camped beneath my neighbor's trees.
Took late-night snacks on his lawn
then mine. I liked their waddle from his maples
to my dogwoods. I liked watching them
dig up my mulch, arming themselves
with fuel. But I knew my neighbor.
I knew their time was limited.

Artichoke Heart

In that stormy dorm room,
the sun broke through a skillet
of clouds and cast an egg yolk
across his face in her kitchenette.

The artichoke heart he boiled
for her smelled like
her mother's kitchen
coated in *ajo* and *chiles,*

and so she stood there
to be served in the small space
he engineered into a cathedral
of lights. But she stopped praying

to anything sunny or divine
years ago and never bit
the sugar skull during
fall holiday, and she couldn't

scrape her teeth into the meat
of this encounter. Despite
the thrill of olive oil. Despite
the green attention paid to her.

Spa Day

My professor told me
even poems
need a spa day.

Their backs need
massaged, their eyes
peeled, their toenails

painted *Purple Palazzo Pants*.
Think of RoMayo's
best buddy, Mercutio,

his poems had a spa day
before the Capulet crash,
before Merc muscled

his way into shenanigans,
into an errant night of bliss,
into the best caution-to-the-wind

scenario Romeo would ever know
and the glance and dance
that saved and destroyed him.

How I Love/Despise Your Instagram Summer

There you are.
In smoking Arkansas.
Your legs dangling
over the lip
of a pickup's bed.

Tanned to the knees
from June's heat wave,
your skin more sand than spray
from the Black River
below the stony bluff

I thought we'd climb
last winter
when the early snow
dampened your auburn hair,
and the forest wept

from a divine force
that stripped oak and farm fields,
leaving in its wake
cow skulls and hips.

Dual Threats

I dazzled
my new lover
at the gym
with three-point
shots and later
in the park
arching
football spirals
in a pickup game.

Beneath the autumn
cheer of oaks,
with aim
at my head
she volleyed
and spiked
the season's
final acorns
and said
one fall
she met
George Plimpton
who signed
her book
and breast.

That was
the last time
she fell
for a dual threat.

History Professor

She proclaimed herself the Whoopi Goldberg
of Westchester Hall. She injected students
with a teeth-knocking adrenaline every Monday
when the campus green still mourned
the death of the weekend.

She liked to leave the podium and circle us up
as she killed with quips about historic figures
we were supposed to admire without question—
the dreadful Jackson and toothy Eleanor,
even JFK wasn't beyond reproach.

She owned a Fox Trotter, stabled at a farm
just outside of town. She rode on Sundays
and said the horse didn't get her jokes.
If she sat in class, it was at the end of the stage,
her knees kicking at the cancer of her past.

Terms

I wish I'd been more kind to you
during the dogwood blooms

of our youth, your quick
hands at all my limbs

throughout first year,
and yet I grew lonely

with the faucet pour of lilacs
beside the bricks

of the AD building,
a sweet, short-lived scent

while you blossomed
full-term like deep May rain.

Constellations

That springtime evening, the Virgo constellation
let go her wheat and blazed a prairie fire across the sky.

We parked inside her streaming, starlit shadows
near the one-room schoolhouse then wandered down

to creek's edge because it was the end of March
and the bugs had not come on. Smooth stones

hummed warm in the blankets of our closed palms
before we skimmed them across the water,

slow and deep. We knew you'd sleep
against your fiancé next week and tell him nothing.

Tell him nothing, our hands empty of rock and river
locked together like the singular spread of waves.

Malus domestica

Tucked in the corner
of the bar, I am deliciously

no one, the smoothest Gala apple
polished like shoes

and left in this alcove
with only my young skin,

taut and tart and unbitten,
still years from middle age

and its gravity of the yard
and cross-pollination.

In the Breezeway

A year after my grandfather died,
I sat with old man Jess in the breezeway
of his ranch home. We rocked
in a glider and listened to the rain.

I searched him for clues about my granddad,
what made him tick, what made him lock his arms
and toll the time those years as the postal clerk,
delivering the best and worst news

to war widows and would-be lovers
miles from home. Jess didn't say much,
his mouth zipped like a tobacco pouch.
I pined to know what these best friends knew.

How deep the rut of war made pathways,
how they returned home to this small town
and stayed quiet friends, pocketing secrets
like this small rain, soft and steady.

Family Reunion

My closest kin gather
to eat more than we should,
pretend not to air out grievances
over my aunt's mashed potatoes
too chunky for most. And when
my cousin stabs the meat like she
nearly stabbed her last boss
and had to slink home to her papa's care,
the room is hushed like cathedral silence.

Will she survive the moment as her fork
glistens, raises up the grayish slab,
while noses sniff the sweat of defeat?
Will the meat find her plate, crowd out
the potato temple, the pyre of green beans?
Will she begin cutting, with knife and fork
in tinny unison, a battle hymn sung in equal parts?

My Grandfather's Concord Wine

Ten years after his passing, the fence still stands.
Old birch he yanked from trips to the Jack's Fork
and wire he culled from hardware store leavings.
Red wine his interest though his wife despaired

such simple pleasures, preferred her bridge games
with shiny Tupperware as emerald as her eyes
and the grasses of Nebraska she still held close
in the small Ozark town they found

a year after the War where both could work
as mechanic and clerk. On Fourth and Main,
their home yielded a garden every year.
Concord grapes grown in August sun still hang

from vines begun so long ago, and I pick them
reaching over the slanted fence, my fingers
purple and grinning from the effort, and plunk
the fruit into buckets as he did, dreaming of wine.

Dusk Walk with My Mother

Tonight we walk the farm, arm in arm,
and choose the winding lane whose middle rises
with humps of fescue still green from late summer rain
that nearly drowned the goats she raises

for milk and cheese, for laughs and destruction.
At the path's end, we find the fence she's never fixed.
The old barb wire slack with age, spotted with rust,
receives the falling light and glows, and I hold her up

while she rests. Past the pines, the brown hills roll
on the land of neighbors loved but rarely spoken to,
and we talk at last about her end, about these
final days—and how we won't hike back just yet.

III.

*Love your neighbor as yourself;
but don't take down the fence.*
—Carl Sandburg

*Is fear comharsa maith
ná mailín airgid.*

*A good neighbor is better
than a bag of money.*
—Connemara saying (from John O'Donohue)

*I want you to be concerned
about your next door neighbor.
Do you know your next door neighbor?*
—Mother Teresa

Yard Sale

after Ted Kooser

At the neighbor's yard sale,
the old woman hawks
chachkies of porcelain girls
and silver schnauzers,
beat-up end tables, Polaroid film,
even tattered paperbacks
from her reading days
when her Army husband
was stationed in Gillenhausen
to protect the West.

Between a German dictionary
and *Hot Money* from Dick Francis
rests my first book. Topped with
basement dust like the others,
the volume does not stand out in
any significant way like those trinkets
or green army men, supine, after a kid
battled to the death. But I do hope
she gets a quarter for my poems.

Olympic Rings

In late summer heat, the young father
blows up a plastic pool on his front lawn.

He's got two kids, tall as school music stands.
They'll love the water no matter its depth.

The papa's cheeks inflate, deflate, like a horn player.
His breath wheezes, hampered by the chore

and the Winston cigarettes. He takes a break
to light one and decorates the air

with Olympic rings. Last winter, he blew
the same art from my front porch

where I handed him a creamed coffee.
He'd dominated a snowball fight

with his boys and won the battle
by toppling the igloo his eldest built.

Took the kid a week, he said. I'm sure
he cried but he blamed the winter wind.

Next Door

A golf caddie would make short work
of the twenty paces of lush green

between my home and the shadow of my neighbor's.
She might squat down and squeeze fingers

inside the blades, perhaps put palms to earth,
feel the savage heartbeat of the earthworm

digging down away from the tiny hooves
of morning robins. She might pluck

a strand of hairy grass, smell it, decipher its age
and height and preferences for rain. The caddie

might learn a lot on that slight hill—
yet remain unaware of the recent past

when I busted my neighbor's basement glass, certain
he harbored some dirty business down there.

Buzzards

They say the evil twists beneath the house,
with a rotten root that rears upward
through the cratered fireplace.
After all, how do you explain
the murder in '79, the kitchen fire
in '86, and the kidnapped boys
back in '55 when nothing like that ever happened?

The Monday morning after Halloween
proves it again: in the street
an opossum rests
mostly tail and head
though she tried to drag herself
back home into the pines.
A breeze delivers the scent of death
mixed with the mealy smell of fallen leaves,
and the buzzards feast on what remains.

Spooked when a lanky jogger passes,
the vultures lift up as one—
synchronized swimmers
in the blue sky. They float
into the five-story pines,
dive into the dark skyward branches,
and wait together at the edge.

The Good Work

The first delight is the soil.

How black loam hugs fingertips,
rubs graciously in the palms like prayer,
falls gently to the earth,
and whispers in this cathedral garden.

I like Sundays here the most
when the town is quiet, the streets
gray and vacant, the trees ripe
with robins and ripped with green arms.

I hoe the tiny rows by hand,
drop the seeds thin as eyelashes
then hide them inside plump mounds
before the rain.

Breakthrough

At the gardeners' conference,
we start indoors. Each apprentice
squared behind a glass partition
because the coronavirus thrives.

One solitary woman,
round like a chickadee,
did not go back to size
after her daughter's birth,

she tells us—could not
with milk and TV
and errands and in-laws.

After lunch, we are meant
for the outdoors, and gardeners
leave books, laptops behind.

The woman's short wings flap at her table,
and many of us want to set her free
and say as much at the doorway.

Yet all we can do is remind her
she must begin by pounding the glass.

Frances

My yoga teacher is a tree
I can't name. More hawthorn
than dogwood, more bark
than bloom—she is the march
of trumpeting cloud banks,
the cranky yellow of the dandelions,
the bullet holes in the shed
from the neighbor kids when their dad
left for good, and I said they could shoot
anything dead, and they pop-pop-popped
the slanting structure while I rose,
no longer throned in *zazen*.

It Ain't Easy at the Top

I want to deny the cat
with baby robin
in its mouth. Refute
its scamper across
the lawn to my feet.

Denounce the quick feline
who leaves what's left
for me, for my royal
nature, I who feed it
tuna on Sundays.

I want to reject this crown,
revive this little bird
to its quaint meanderings
from maple to hedge,
but the throne won't budge.

Shaq Dancing

Quarantined, I wonder:

What if memes
become true feelings,

this is how I love you,
Shaq dancing,

this is how I miss you,
Shaq dancing,

this is how I despise you,
Shaq dancing,

this is how I missed your life
unfold in front of me,

that blood Lotus opening
honey honey honey

in the Japanese garden,

how I think
we blushed
and raked the sand,

how I think
surely we blushed
and raked the sand,

Shaq dancing.

How to Lose Weight during a Pandemic

1) Start your day with protein.
Yoga, egg, cheese.

2) Swim in a saltwater pool.
Do laps; don't just float.

3) Eat chips and guac for lunch.
No extra salt.

4) Drink away the afternoon on the deck.
Apply tanning lotion; read fiction.

5) Order delivery or takeout.
Enjoy a small serving; save the rest.

6) Think about those you've lost.
Open the window but don't jump.

7) Stay up late.
Fuck and fuck some more.

White Dwarf Star: A Love Poem

Such a bright star—you punctured
the northern sky with fire.

Loosed upon the earth in light,
you built wood decks, mapped out

new city streets, fed the meth-head
who crashed in the woods near Fourth,

guided your mother's hands over insulin
daggers, and spoke my love language

of time spent. Then. The gravity of undone dishes,
the fractured soffit rusted by rain pour, the child

who didn't take. Until.

We let it all go. The daughter, the calendar,
the house efforts, expectations. Then.

The glow from our kitchen—lamp light
in golden orbit, casting the filaments

of the unknown onto our dark lawn.

Forgotten Ice Cube Tray on the Counter

August lava pours
through the kitchen windows,
runs down the sink,
bubbles in the dishwasher
and commands the floor.
My wife and I stand
fixed in the fiery loam.

At the freezer, she fingers
an ice cube tray, cracks it
into a pair of tumblers.
She slices a lime and pours the rest
of the vodka, patting its rump
for good measure.

We don't speak,
just raise glasses in toast.
Then she takes off her shirt,
her pants, and, barefoot, thumps away
while calling my name.

Pie

On my morning walk, a pair of robins bicker and bite,
one small snack away from making love
or becoming tree-top enemies
where sight is more important than food.

One takes off, loses the other in a whisk of wings
and stirs a moment in the pines—alone—
in a deep quiet, like an oven doing its lonesome work
before the meringue is burnt to a crisp.

Young Couple

The young couple down the street
moved out; moved out so well

no one noticed. Except if one observed
the extra trash last Monday.

Today, cardboard boxes no longer impale
the overgrown grass and corner peonies.

It's the first time the carport is cleaned.
Gone is the broken baby highchair,

shadowed in cobwebs. Gone is
the slumped camping table and cook stove.

Gone is the Amy Winehouse on repeat
booming down the alley.

Colorado Wildflower Seed Mix

Will the seed take? Cast in
the shaded alcove and down
the narrow patch I've hauled
lawn refuse, mown crabgrass
and dandelions, and dead
oak limbs.

In this shade is the site of the dead,
opossum spines and buzzard droppings,
dark circles ribbed with white,
from the wake that never sleeps.

Here I am shirtless, with this bag
of seeds in doomsday August,
booted feet on this thin path, dreaming of
new flowers, petrified of the looming
divorce, of these Colorado blooms
that just might take.

Brown Recluse

So misunderstood, you.
With the ferociously long
legs and the violin tattoo.
Such symmetry & poise
& history. Your toxin
bred from bacteria, the fodder
of God to keep things

on equal footing. But the Almighty
couldn't divine the real matter
below your rigid skin—
that beautiful, dark instinct—
as I could not, when young,
unsure of the benefits
of tight, measured corners.

When Children Need Another Player
and the Smallest Boy Asks

I nod because yes is the only answer.
From the NBA three-point line,
his mighty scrawniness launches
the do-or-die shot to mark who will get
the ball first. When his air ball dives, he laughs,
and so does everyone else.

When the smooth leather comes my way,
I pass to the low post without looking.
The ball thumps a tween's chest but he lays it in.
When passed to again, I shoot a rocket
from thirty foot that swishes through the net,
and I laugh, and so does everyone else.

IV.

*You know, during all those years away
there were a few things I missed not being here.
I missed knowing that nothing ever changes,
people never change. It makes you feel
real solid.*
—Myra Fleener, *Hoosiers*

Bypass

The bypass forms a half moon
around our sleepy town
and its unlit drama. Night-time
travelers lose themselves
in the neon of a pair of box stores,
a line of fast-food restaurants.

Some stop. Others just turn
heads back to the wide four-lane
that will take them to the thick
of Jonesboro or Memphis.
I never cross at the big light
where the new Hilton rests

large and gray on the bare ridge.
I take the hilly back road
where deer graze in early November,
scared up from the hunters
to the south. They bounce
across the blacktop in two leaps

like the country dance,
quick-quick slow-slow,
into the autumn dawn
where they forage for broadleaf
while the town lights
blink into being.

Night Snow in April

The night is black and full.
The town sleeps in the valley,
a silent garden, where pear and apple
shutter their naked blooms.
Before buzzard or crow wake,

it begins to snow. Creamy flakes
fall, the rich dark deepens, this can't
be April one thinks, but the whole
town is covered like this, black
and white.

Sailing Elsewhere

At the snowy grave site, the preacher asks
if anyone wishes to add words.
A woman rises while the tent flaps pop
like lightning able to char the nearby oaks
she once climbed as a girl.

In the clearing just her, a frail woman,
grayed into winter hay, and she declares
this dead aunt is the only one who really
loved her, who piggybacked her
across her father's drunken torso
weekends spilled on the kitchen floor.

This aunt ferried her across the broken bridge
at the navy base, across Hades, across familiar corpses.
She was the one, this beloved relative
docked in the casket, who betrayed her now,
sailing elsewhere without her.

Casts

In our town, the insurance man
boasts six generations deep. He attended
vo-tech school before dropping out
when he sparked more fires than finished pipes.

To keep my file up to date, he mails too much homework
like the shop teacher assigning more reading than machining.
From time to time, I see him at high school football games
bonded to his seat among the boosters.

He doesn't know me down near the field,
where I anchor like a ship's fillet weld,
casting my iron opinion to stone-faced refs
for all to hear.

Town Lion, Standing Room Only

The ugly stick got broke on him
and blasted into a damn lot of pieces
like in movies when cars crash
through wood buildings
near urban river docks.

Yet he wore the grotesque
like a badge of honor.
He never donned hats,
sported shaving cuts,
preferred cheap cologne
far below his pay grade.

For forty years, he taught
high school rebels and outcasts
the miracle of engines in automotive class.
He gave short speeches at the Lion's,
delivered meals on wheels without fanfare,
and when no one was looking, he saved
the downtown shops from box stores,
just months before he died.

Flood

On the park bench,
the young man waits
for her. Twice his age
reveals poor math,
he thinks to himself.

Her black lab appears.
Then she stage right.
Her ankles sing opera
above the trimmed lawn.
She smells of garlic and rosemary.
Shadow sniffs his leg
until yanked into submission.

Chance rain strikes all three of them
through the walnut branches.
The man keeps his eyes open
inside the flood. Her fingers wet,
the leash slips.

Big Muddy

When a girl, she bicycled down
to the wharf and made up tales
about her ancestors, the French
fur-trader who drank the Mississippi
with a spoon and crafted a canoe
out of silver and the coats of owls,
generously given upon the quarter-century
deaths of the barred variety.

And here she is again.
On the banks of the Big Muddy,
divorced and dried-out,
lying belly up, more opossum
than girl now, her chipped-polish toes
baking like meat.

She finds someone's empty pint, flings
boozy dew drops into a wide open
mouth. Then she grabs a thin piece
of driftwood and stretches it out
like an animal skin, trying to reach

her found flip-flop, hooked
in an abandoned fishing net,
with flashing hollows that look like eyes,
she thinks, like the brown ones
of her man's lover she never dreamed
he'd take.

I Love the Little Maple

I love the little maple
at the edge of the woods.
Modest and unassuming
like the town priest,
the tree wears
an autumn robe
of crimson stars
and says little.

Above the village,
the wind blows
through the ridge
and batters tall pines
and their big ideas
of standing here forever.

Naked, the hefty oaks
bend with creaking knees
while this slight maple
still blooms
orange and burgundy,
its stems deep red
like blood.

Soccer Field

A former lover turned
old and then she died.
How could she?

The summer she was
forty, we climbed
Taum Sauk Mountain
with little more steam
than a pair of granola bars
and a bag of trail mix.

And now her hiking legs
are drained of blood,
the tiny hairs
above her knees
growing in some morgue
without me to skim
them like cream.

And that laugh
is gone, stitched
behind a shade of
blue lips as the
mortuary man
takes hold
of that drowsy head
of fluffy brown,

like the autumn leaves
outside my window,
mulched underfoot
by the teenagers
who cut through
my lawn
to the soccer field.

Minutes from Signing the Papers

They lingered in the street
in front of their lawn she'd just trimmed,

in front of the flowerbeds he'd just weeded,
and the breeze smelled of their labor,

tangy grass and azalea spice.
Sweaty and silent beside their bicycles,

they knew they leaned one ride away
from signing the papers,

from licking a gummy envelope
destined for some divorce lawyer

two hundred miles away in Kansas City.
They put feet to pedals and spun them,

a dull clicking that set off a brood of cicadas
who deafened the neighborhood.

They spoke in tandem for a moment
but couldn't hear each other over the din.

Dr. Abbott

Gaunt like the town pines she walks beneath,
she wears white blouses with tan slacks,
her casual wear on Fridays
back when she taught the classics,
and everyone called her doctor per her order.

After all, a former housewife saves
her grocery bill change, affords night school,
and wins a scholarship at an esteemed program—
without a doubt she earned the honorific.

Now, she flutters from sidewalk to sidewalk
like leafy pages in a Shakespeare volume
popping in the wind. If you stop her on the street,
she won't lecture you on *Hamlet*
or wearing white after Labor Day
because she's already forgotten the lesson
before it's even started.

Daycare Playground

Seated in a folding chair,
the woman, barely in her twenties,
suns legs with ankles propped
on the anchored mini-motorcycle.

She ignores the other monitor
who tries to share TikToks
and relationship advice.
The kids scream and claw
while burned-out mufflers
from the street silence no one.

A male cardinal lands
on the building's gutter.
His song is pretty, she thinks,
with all those same alto notes.
Too pretty really. But she's too
tired to bend down and throw
a stone.

Swing

The swing the boy hung beneath the deck
doesn't move in this morning's breeze.

It's locked in time in space
like Legos and astronauts he built
on vacant afternoons.

And empty, too, like hotels,
like his teenage heart
gouged by his father's absence—

the littering of jobs that breezed him
in and out of the child's life.

In Two Years' Time

He'll glide home from college.
What will move him most?
His mother's small brown eyes,
more like acorns than the autumn
walnuts he remembers.

Or the A-frame shed.
That piece of shit held together
only by his will—his late-night
devotion, the trumpeting of wood screws
into his latest hardwood creation,
the desk, the table, the altar.

Or his dad's roguish smile he missed
most days because he was a teenager
and a boy bent on becoming a man
not like his father, like his father.

V.

*Life and death are the only issues;
we often forget that—
arranging our furniture,
washing our cars.*
—Diane Wakoski

*Your skin does not separate you
from the world. It is a bridge
through which the external world
flows into you. And you flow into it.*
—Alan Watts

Driving Years Later

The Flint Hills roll out before me
like an emerald carpet though I remember

the knolls longer, taller, more dark and mysterious
than these simple stitches quilted beneath

an orange thimble. Night will come on shortly,
and coyotes will talk in voices

I recall from adolescence. In this country,
I held my innocence in my palm

longer than most, like how one scoops water
from a stream, how bubbles climb and disappear

over clenched fingers, and you drink
until you lose your breath.

One Minute Read

for P.H.

Last Christmas, he was still alive.
A Duck Duck Go search tells me so.

And now.
The online obit.

1 min read.

329 words
make up his life.

Voted "favorite prof"
by his students

time and time again.
No one knows

about the grace
he gave me, the keys

to his writing cabin
in the woods. Mine

for a summer while he
faked back pain

to convince his spouse
I should go, not he.

Over the fire stove
I built from rebar,

I cooked rice and beans,
ate small game.

Near the creek
I built a shower

and wooed
a laughing lover

there. It felt like
infinity with her

bathing that summer.
I wish he could have known.

Meditation on Fifty

Now you won't ever *not*
be in pain—take the arthritic
legs of the magnolia, spread
long and knotty, femur
to fibula, then nicked
on Sundays by the mower,
the searing grind
like a sermon where God
is love and less so
in Nature, in the magnolia
root where darkness
still dwells, calling itself
the unknown.

After I Disappointed a Friend

More grizzly now than man,
he rumbles in the deep forest.
Pines thick at his shoulders,
even the breeze fears to move
through such tight spaces.

In the evening light,
on all fours, he thrashes
against spring's undergrowth,
and his furry head waves white
like river foam.

He won't venture to the water
where I linger, just a lone fisherman.
But I call out to him while
the season's salmon dart away
from every single streamer I toss.

What There Is to Know about the Human Heart

I did not know a partially formed heart
beat within this chest. Thin veins,
loose valves, a wild beating, more murmur

than pump. Mounting craggy hills
on the farm, fixing fence in August hell,
enduring hornet stings from their groundswell—

all this theater ran for many years
until the sick summer when I couldn't walk
like the days before, couldn't work

like the years before—a plague in chest
and limb. In the fall, the forest
welcomed me to stroll though the pain

had not left with summer heat,
and this heart beat faster, larger,
as if for every living thing.

Symmetry

Far from the woods I savor,
in the grocery parking lot,
tiny wrens and fierce grackles
scrap for burger remains

without song, just near-silent
hopping and occasional screeches
outside my car window
where I've parked west of them

after a failed trip to the dentist—
my volcanic gums a mystery,
my seismic jaw, too—
and right now there is only

the ink-blue sky above a plague
of grocery carts, linked beak
to beak, where a boy muscles them,
humming dreamy lyrics to a pop song.

Cooking for a New Friend

Last week she turned fifty
within a life unknown to me.
I can only guess at the ways
she's travelled, given the scar
on her forearm,

the photos on the fridge:
the beach with a brother,
Spain with a sister,
a French uncle who died young
from AIDS she said the night

I cooked mung dal and she recounted
her trip with him to India,
to a temple in Kannur
where priest and ritual
burned a morning into being.

Her Freckled Face Seen in a Batch of Bananas

I never add notes to my pickup order,
but how much I want to add:

Pick green bananas, please,
but I figure they've got a shit job

to start with and don't need
my preferences for fruit.

Today, I get mushy ones picked
three days past fresh.

Deep yellow, they have grown specks
overnight and now rest in the dawn light

all freckled and beautiful, like Carrie
from grade school, endlessly teased

for being spotted and red-haired,
her gaze always turned to the sun.

Warn Your Doctor If You Get a Parasitic Infection When Taking This Drug

Let this warning
be a warning to you
when gulping
down the pill
destined to cure
your eczema woes.

Remember first:
Don't eat apples, blueberries,
spinach or kale.
Don't consume kefir
or tempeh.
And for god's sake,
don't grow your own food.

Drink a good chunk
of chorine water
with this pill.
No need to mediate
or pray
or Louise Hay this thing
with the power
of positive thinking.

Get real.

Skins

Each night of sleep we shed the skin
of yesterday. In twilight hours, the sky
unfolds blue light from the stars again
like a child who takes her paper plane
straight back to formula to begin once more
simply because. The crickets saw their song
like carpenters planing birch to a perfect pitch.
The robins, once quiet, chirp their awakening.

Autumn Float

We make the gravel bar before dusk.
Our kayaks groan with as much
wearied muscle as our own.
Fire is first, and driftwood disappears
in air as blue flame then ash.

We decide against tents,
those nylon slivers made to resist
evening wind and rain.
We would rather face the flood
of stars above the bluff.

After fish and scotch and fire,
sleeping bags form around us
while we chat then stop
because the river shares a secret

in a low constant whoosh
that hushes owl and coyote,
and ushers us
into the arms of slumber.

Drinking Near Dark

A finger of bourbon is all
I drink these days. No matter
the winter weather—when the snow
holds the most mystery
in its simple white slip,

more ghost than human
when flakes brush near
my burning cheeks
and glide past the hips
of the wheelbarrow
to disappear beneath the magnolia.

When dark eats up the valley,
I am still holding
the smallest of tumblers,
no fingers but fumes, until
there's no light at all.

Evening Walk

During my evening walk, the sun burns
above the Ozark hills—an oil lantern

on top of the knobs, with a glow
as deep as an autumn pumpkin.

The auburn heart grazes just above
the brown, rolling ridges

I've loved like old friends.
I tread the woods

as the lilting beams warm
the arms of shortleaf pines.

Beside the pond, bull frogs chuckle
about some long-held joke.

My feet, hardly my own now, touch down
on a stranded bed of pine needles.

Bury Me

Bury me on that hill
where the old farm lay,
where dusk fires orange
where the grasses sport red tops,
and the headstones wear gray.

Bury me on that land
the Confederates took then lost.
Build a circle garden
round about my stone.
Promise to plant short flowers
that don't cover my marker
with a phrase I've yet to think of.

Promise you'll trick me, promise
you'll agree to pansies, but sow lilies
instead. Make them stargazer or tiger.
Let them crowd out my legacy, my plans,
and dance a lifetime in the dusk.

Country Farmhouses Like Mine

Across the pasture, the robin's morning song
a dart through the open window. Rousing,
I rustle flannel sheets to chin and cast eyes
wide open to a smoky field of fescue.

Silence takes a turn, fills up space
reserved within country farmhouses like mine.
Skunks have traveled nighttime miles
to bunk beneath the shaded porch while katydids

bloom quiet in the oaks and elms.
When I rise, what I've inherited
becomes blood, the red stretch of corn
surrounding me as I beat the eggs.

About the Author

Dave Malone is a poet and writer from the Missouri Ozarks. He holds degrees from Ottawa University and Indiana State University. A three-time Pushcart nominee, he is the author of eight volumes of poetry. His other books include *Tornado Drill* (Aldrich Press, 2022), *You Know the Ones* (Golden Antelope Press, 2017), and *View from the North Ten* (Mongrel Empire Press, 2013). He can be found online at *davemalone.net* or on Instagram *@dave.malone*.

www.ingramcontent.com/pod-product-compliance
Lightning Source LLC
Chambersburg PA
CBHW030052170426
43197CB00010B/1487